PAUL STRAND

PAUL STRAND

A RETROSPECTIVE MONOGRAPH
THE YEARS 1915–1946

AN APERTURE BOOK

1972

DEDICATION

TO JACOB STRAND, MY FATHER,
WHOSE FAITH IN MY WORK NEVER FALTERED
FROM ITS BEGINNINGS TO THE
TIME OF HIS DEATH IN 1949.
WHEN PHOTOGRAPHY AS AN ART MEDIUM
WAS STILL NEW AND UNACCEPTED,
HE DID NOT DOUBT ITS POSSIBILITIES
NOR QUESTION HIS SON'S
CHOICE OF A LIFE WORK.
THIS FAITH, SO SIMPLE AND CLEAR,
IS REFLECTED IN THIS BOOK.

This book is set in Linofilm Baskerville by
Poole Clarinda Company, printed by
Rapoport Printing Corporation, and bound by
Kingsport Press. The paper, Lustro Offset Dull,
is manufactured by S. D. Warren Company.
The design is by Peter Bradford.

The photographs were selected, sequenced, and sized
by Paul Strand, Hazel Strand, and Michael Hoffman.
An edition bound as one volume has been
produced by Aperture, Inc. and published
to accompany a major retrospective exhibition
by the Philadelphia Museum of Art,
City Art Museum of St. Louis,
Boston Museum of Fine Arts,
Metropolitan Museum of Art,
Los Angeles County Museum of Art,
M. H. DeYoung Memorial Museum of San Francisco.
An edition bound in two volumes is published
by Aperture, Inc. for general distribution.

Aperture, Inc. is a non-profit, educational
organization publishing a Quarterly of Photography,
portfolios, and books to communicate with
serious photographers and creative people everywhere.
Address: Elm Street, Millerton, New York 12546

PUBLICATIONS COMMITTEE: Minor White, Editor
Michael E. Hoffman, Managing Editor-Publisher
Stevan A. Baron, Production Advisor
William E. Parker, Editorial Consultant
Arthur M. Bullowa   Shirley C. Burden

TABLE OF CONTENTS
VOLUME I

ACKNOWLEDGEMENTS

The material of the past fifty years and the selection of photographs and text for this monograph have made me aware of the many people who have helped during the growth and evolution of my work.

These many friends are present here: those who knowingly or unknowingly opened roads of purpose and opportunity which led me to new work, those whose responses to my photographs often gave me more clarity of purpose and a measure of achievement, and not least those who were the subjects of the photographs. I wish to acknowledge the presence of each and all in this book.

In the actual making of the monograph, my thanks to Walter and Naomi Rosenblum for their help in 1964 in the early stages of structure and montage. My appreciation to Catherine Duncan who has played a key role in the editing of the text. With infinite patience she has gone through many revisions, additions, subtractions, rejections, and discoveries. To Michael Hoffman my appreciation for his creative work in regard to every aspect of the realization of the book.

In 1965 my friends Beaumont and Nancy Newhall suggested to Michael Hoffman that he arrange a meeting to discuss publication by Aperture of my photographs. At that time my work—which had been shown by Alfred Stieglitz and published in two numbers of *Camera Work*, published in *20 Photographs of Mexico* in 1940, shown at the Museum of Modern Art in 1945, published in *Time in New England* in 1950—was no longer well known except to students of photography. Few in America knew of the extent of my work published and unpublished which began in 1950 in France and continued in Italy, the Outer Hebrides, Egypt, Ghana, Morocco, and Rumania. As a result of my meeting with Michael Hoffman and consequent collaboration the idea of a major exhibition and publication developed. Evan Turner, Director, and Kneeland McNulty, Curator of Prints and Drawings, of the Philadelphia Museum of Art were enthusiastic about both projects. With their generous support and advice, this retrospective monograph and the exhibition which it accompanies had a firm beginning. The participation of the City Art Museum of St. Louis, Boston Museum of Fine Arts, Metropolitan Museum of Art, Los Angeles County Museum of Art, and the M. H. DeYoung Memorial Museum of San Francisco assured the making of the monograph and exhibition.

I wish to acknowledge with thanks the work of Peter C. Bunnell, Curator of Photography of the Museum of Modern Art, for insuring the completeness and accuracy of the Bibliography; the assistance of Minor White, William E. Parker, Arthur M. Bullowa, Stevan A. Baron for making creative suggestions as the book developed; the work of Peter Bradford for his thoughtful and distinguished design; and the cooperation of Sidney Rapoport who labored on the press to make each reproduction as true to the original print as possible. *Paul Strand*

Photography has been Paul Strand's life. It is the instrument through which he has penetrated deep recesses of nature and people, the instrument by means of which he has conveyed to the world what the keenest eye has seen, what the livest sensitivity has felt, what the most passionate sympathy has cried out to say. It is the language in which he has written the most eloquent modern paean to the strength and dignity of man, to the brooding violence and beauty of nature. . . .

Photography is very easy. The visible world is such an interesting place that it doesn't take much in the way of passion, insight, sensitivity, or rigorous craft to make a picture worth looking at—at least briefly. But photography is very difficult. The visible world is so harshly recalcitrant. It stays where it is in its own context. It takes the quickest eye, the most penetrating insight, and the most painstaking technique to make a photograph that is a felt comment, bare of inessentials; a photograph that moves the viewer with an understanding of the meaning of what is photographed.

What I hope this work may do for audience and photographers alike is to reveal clearly again the source of the great tradition in photography which began with David Octavius Hill, continued in the great bodies of work of Atget and Stieglitz, and which has reached its fullest expression in the work of Paul Strand. These are the sources of all

great art: passion, the integration of its materials within its ideas, and the profound obligation to the truths and abundance of experience.

. . . No picture of Strand's is brilliant for brilliance's sake. To him the object is all important. His photograph is his best effort to render the emotional significance of the object. His approach is one of utmost simplicity. In this sense his photographs are impersonal, selfless; yet they are characterized by a strong emotion.

He has sought in his photographs to express his most vigorous feelings about his world. His passion has sharpened his vision to the degree where he is satisfied with no less than the most dramatic manifestation of events. It has driven him to the most superb mastery of techniques, so that his medium places no impediment to his expression. And as a result he has opened a new world to photography and through it rendered revelations into human experience. He has written an autobiography of himself in terms of the things he has seen. He has given us photographs that are more than the look and the surface of things, photographs that live and grow, that will take on new beauty and meaning for people as long as his prints and these superb reproductions are seen. *Leo Hurwitz in the Foreword,* The Mexican Portfolio, *1940 & 1967.*

This number of *Camera Work* is devoted entirely to the new work of Paul Strand. The last number too was devoted in part to Strand's photographs. In it we wrote: . . . "291" exhibitions are never exhibitions in the ordinary sense, but a series of experiments and demonstrations, all interrelated. During the International at the Armory (1913) it was but logical for "291" to show the Stieglitz photographs. Likewise it was the logical step in the evolution of "291" exhibitions to show photographs during the Forum Show. And to show pure photographs. No photographs had been shown at "291" in the interim, primarily because "291" knew of no work outside of Paul Strand's which was worthy of "291." None outside of his had been done by any new worker in the United States for some years, and as far as is our knowledge none had been done in Europe during that time. By new worker, we do not mean new picture maker. . . . New picture makers happen every day, not only in photography, but also in painting. New picture makers are notoriously nothing but imitators of the accepted; the best of them imitators of, possibly at one time, original workers. For ten years Strand quietly had been studying, constantly experimenting, keeping in close touch with all that is related to life in its fullest aspect; intimately related to the spirit of "291." His work is rooted in the best traditions of photography. His vision is potential. His work is pure. It is direct. It does not rely upon tricks of process. In whatever he does there is applied intelligence. In the history of photography there are but few photographers who, from the point of view of expression, have really done work of any importance. And by importance we mean work that has some relatively lasting quality, that element which gives all art its real significance.

The photogravures in this number represent the real Strand. The man who has actually done something from within. The photographer who has added something to what has gone before. The work is brutally direct. Devoid of all flim-flam; devoid of trickery and of any "ism;" devoid of any attempt to mystify an ignorant public, including the photographers themselves. These photographs are the direct expression of today. *Alfred Stieglitz in* Camera Work, *1917.*

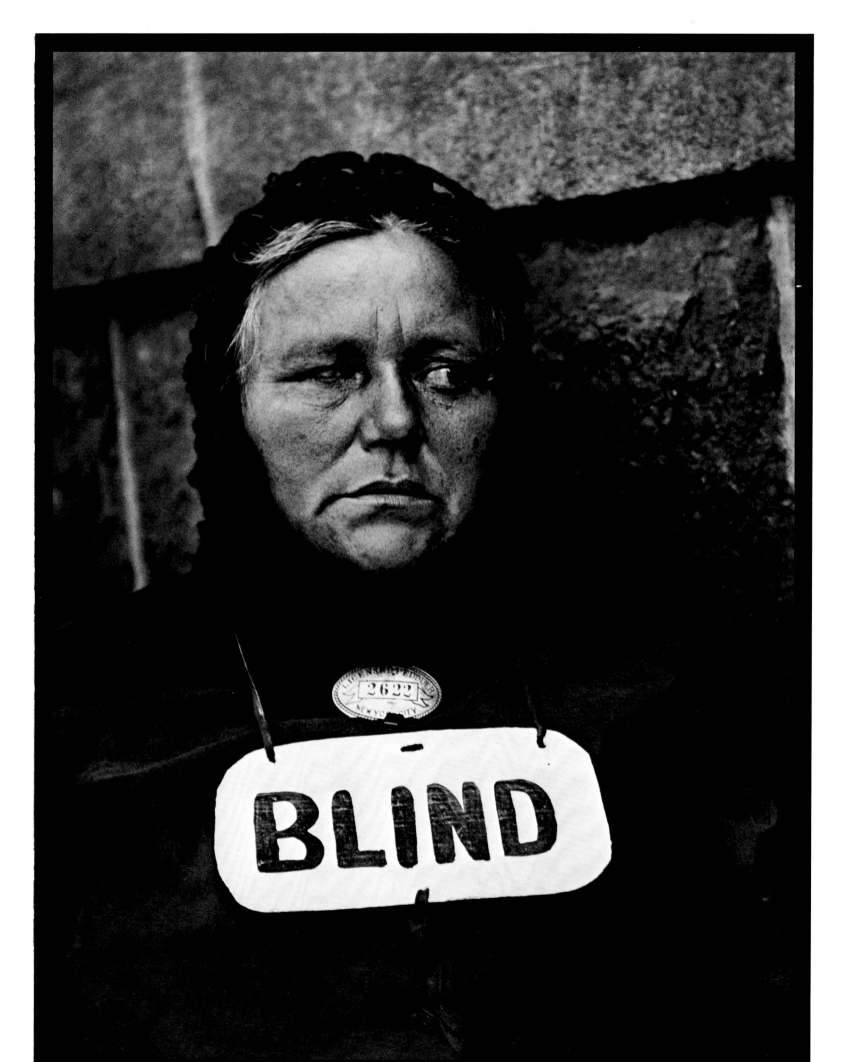

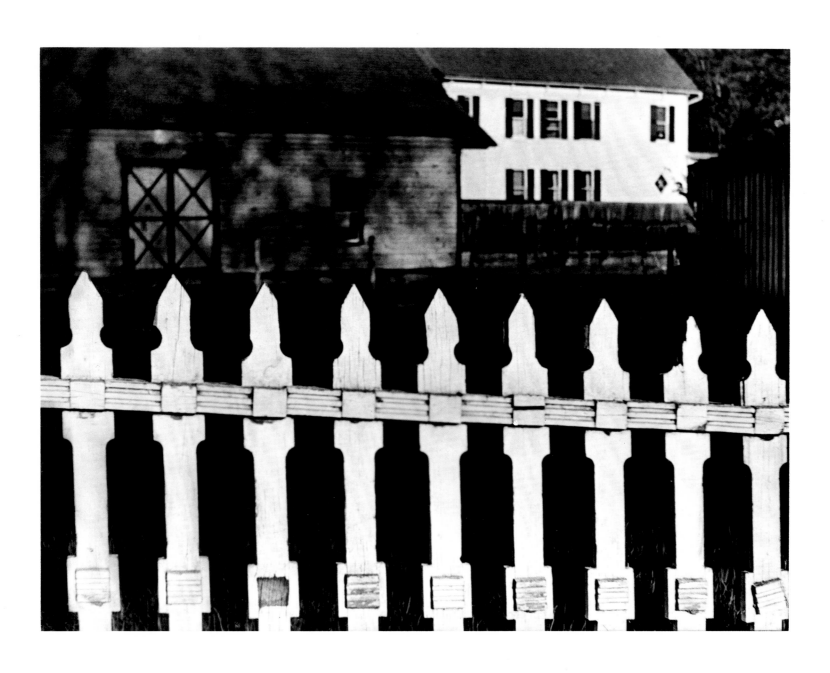

Photography, which is the first and only important contribution thus far of science to the arts, finds its raison d'être, like all media, in a complete uniqueness of means. This is an absolute unqualified objectivity. . . .

The photographer's problem, therefore, is to see clearly the limitations and at the same time the potential qualities of his medium, for it is precisely here that honesty, no less than intensity of vision, is the prerequisite of a living expression. This means a real respect for the thing in front of him, expressed in terms of chiaroscuro through a range of almost infinite tonal values which lie beyond the skill of human hand. The fullest realization of this is accomplished, without tricks of process or manipulation, through the use of straight photographic methods. It is in the organization of this objectivity that the photographer's point of view toward life enters in, and where a formal conception born of the emotions, the intellect, or of both is as inevitably necessary for him before an exposure is made as for the painter before he puts brush to canvas. . . . Photography is only a new road from a different direction, but moving toward the common goal, which is life.

The existence of a medium, after all, is its absolute justification if, as so many seem to think, it needs one; and all comparison of potentialities is useless and irrelevant. Whether a watercolor is inferior to an oil, or whether a drawing, an etching, or a photograph is not as important as either is inconsequent. To have to despise something in order to respect something is a sign of impotence. Let us rather accept joyously and with gratitude everything through which the spirit of man seeks to an ever fuller and more intense self-realization. *Paul Strand in* Seven Arts, *1917.*

. . . Paul Strand's original, unaffected, straightforward photographs of 1915-1916 . . . brought a new vision to photography, discovering in the most ordinary objects significant forms full of aesthetic appeal. Nearly all his pictures broke new ground both in subject matter and in its presentation. The white fence running across the entire width of the picture intentionally destroys all sense of perspective. The bowls and other experiments in abstraction were the result of Strand's seeing at "291" the work of Picasso, Braque, Brancusi, and others.

From a letter by Paul Strand to Helmut Gernsheim . . . "I was trying to apply their then strange abstract principles to photography in order to understand them. Once understanding what the aesthetic elements of a picture were, I tried to bring this knowledge to objective reality in the "White Fence," the "Viaduct," and other New York photographs. Nor have I ever returned to pure abstraction, as it had no further meaning for me in itself. On the other hand, subject matter all around me seemed inexhaustible. I began to explore the close-up. The portraits of people in New York streets represent another trend in experimentation: This was to photograph people without their being conscious of being photographed. The technique I used at the time was a false lens screwed to the side of my 3¼" x 4¼" reflex camera."

Strand's New York street scenes and characters and other everyday subjects are wonderfully alive, fragments of the kaleidescopic variety of appearances which are so familiar that one is apt to overlook their photographic potentialities. They owe their vitality and expressiveness to the photographer's personal taste and artistic knowledge, showing the facts filtered through the subjectivity of the artist. Yet what makes these photographs so striking is their apparent objectivity. . . . Paul Strand was bringing back the original but long forgotten conception of photography.

. . . The first to proclaim the doctrine of objectivity, Strand developed its potentialities from 1921 onward by concentrating on the magnificent forms . . . in the machine, close-ups of plants, time-withered trees, driftwood, and rock formations. *Helmut Gernsheim in* Creative Photography, *1960.*

March 31/29.

Dear Strand; There was a middle-aged man in this afternoon. For over an hour. I read. He looked. Walked around the Room several times — examined every photograph minutely — & at a distance. Grew visibly excited. Finally blurted out: "this is a great experience for me. I suppose very few really see what's there." — He sat down — and continued looking. I finally asked him where he was born. — Sweden — 20 years in America — scenic manager of a theatre on B'way & 44th Street. Used to photograph himself — Metol poisoning stopped him. Saw the sign "photographs" & he said: When one once has photography in the blood — it sticks. — Said also has seen virtually no good photography in years. A real person. — I enjoyed his intense enjoyments. Masculine type. —

I'm afraid you have misunderstood many things I have said during your show. —

Your old ——— S.

34

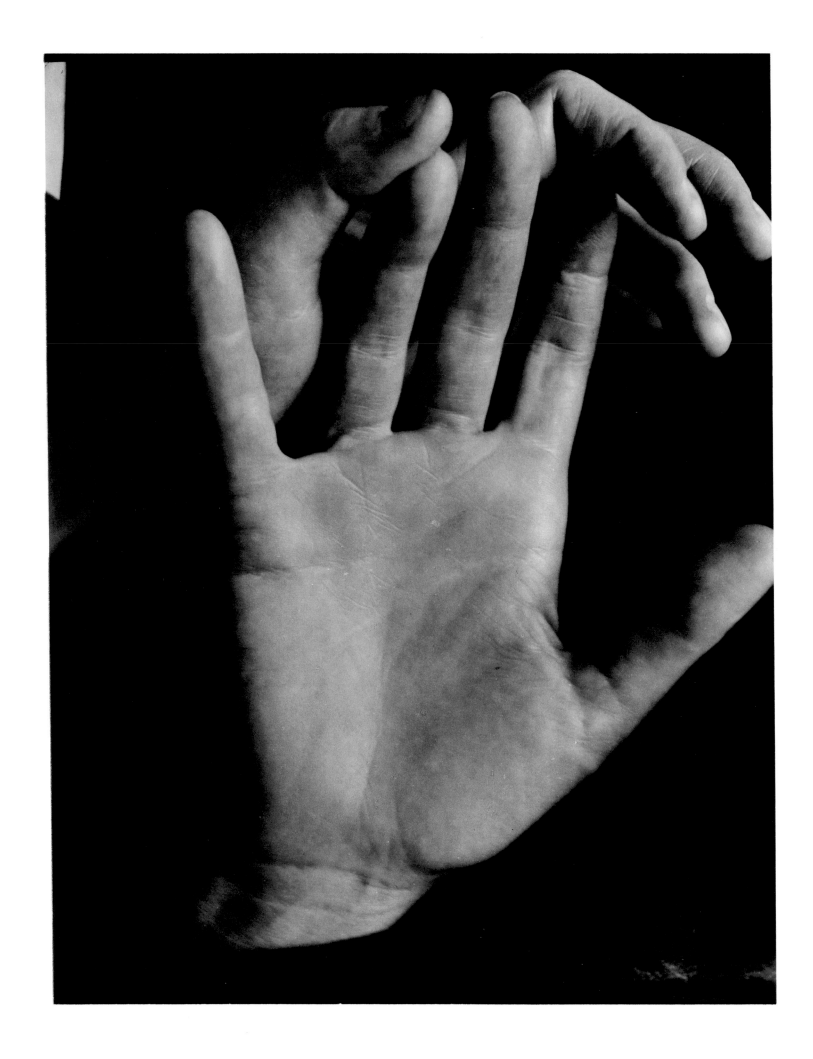

MACHINE AND NATURE FORMS

. . . These photographs are not cold. Their marvelous texture, which is one of their most immediately striking traits, is not merely a matter of technical finish or a superimposed gloss, but the manifestation of a particular form of sensibility. The artist by a sort of sensuous sympathy with the body of his material has somehow become one with it; so that the Strand machine seems not only the perfect image of a machine, but of a machine that in some mysterious way has itself become conscious of its own admirable and independent life, its own elegance of line, suave hardness, and density of substance. The machine looks out upon us calmly exultant in the knowledge of its own consummate organism. *Harold Clurman in* Creative Art, *1929*.

. . . in late 1917 Strand made a photograph restricted to the wheel and related parts of a car. In tracing the development of the machine as a motif, no other photograph has been discovered that anticipated this close-up of a machine form. While machines have been photographed from the earliest years of photography, never before was this done in an aesthetic context.

Strand, in recalling his print of the wheel complex on a Lozier car, recently wrote that this picture, along with his photographs of details of kitchen bowls, a shadow on a porch, and a white picket fence, while being abstract experiments, actually led him to a greater awareness of the objective world. . . . It seems very true that Strand was never interested in design *per se* or any other part of formalism but that his principle interest was and has continued to be man and the world in which he lives and what he creates in that world. *Van Deren Coke*

The subject matter of the photograph is the inside of a motion picture camera. Study the tonality, look at the scale of gradation, look at the print color, and you will then begin to see some of photography's potential. Look at how beautifully the lens draws the subject, look at the way in which the forms are organized, how the edges of the photograph disappear because of the way in which the photographer has organized its surface. It is a quiet photograph, not dependent on the excitement of bizarre subject matter. Strand is paying homage to a machine made by man, to the beauties inherent in its shape, its form. This photograph is a perfect marriage of content to form. *Walter Rosenblum*

The intangible but unerring forces of Nature, the faint perfume that guides the bee to the honey sac, the quiet beginnings of day and of life, the things, in short, that poets regard as the great essentials are the matters that Paul Strand seeks to record with the instrument that above all others has been held responsible for the disillusionment of modern life — the camera. . . .

A cobweb in the rain! Fancy photographing that! Yet who that has ever watched a spider engaged in its marvelous task of web-building but has felt a stab at the heart, bewildered at the spider craftsmanship that implies age-old apprenticeships. And the rich spongy fungi that spring up in the woods overnight at about this season of the year, and the crisscross patterns of the withered beach grasses that have fascinated Chinese artists for centuries, and the time-eaten surfaces of ancient rocks that have been bitten by the wind and rain into hieroglyphics that seem to mean everything — these are the themes Paul Strand plays on with a camera that is never allowed for a moment to assume the upper role. *Henry McBride in* New York Sun, *1929.*

These photographs leave me with an overwhelming sense of the organic life of the objects they depict. Plants, stones, the age-old fragments of trees, all appear as the living parts of some vast and moving whole that seems through them to have drawn measurably nearer. These growths, taken up close against the eye of the camera and showing the intricate and delicate structure of their plant-bones through the downy flesh of the leaves, seem breathing through all their pores. One thinks of their elements as dissolving and sinking back into the earth but to reform and put forth again from the full seed—but never of their final dissolution; the Strand world is one in which there is no death as the children of Adam regard it. . . . The aspects of the outer world that he has here presented have been apprehended by the inner as well as by the outer eye and the mechanical one of the camera. These objects are not isolated from their universe but profoundly related to it. *Lola Ridge in* Creative Art, *1931*.

The work of Paul Strand has become a legend. . . . Time and again photographers coming in brief contact with its force and its extraordinary beauty have felt the shock of a catalyst. Strand has been a discoverer of photographic forms and concepts for our time, penetrating with unswerving logic and passion through each succeeding phase of his problem. . . . In 1929 Strand went to the Gaspé . . . where he began composing with all landscape elements, developing an exquisite sense for the moment when the moving forces of clouds, people, boats are in perfect relation with the static forms of houses and headlands. In this little series, where the whites blaze in the cold light of the North, that sense of spirit of place which is implicit in the New York and Maine series emerges as the dominant theme of Strand's work. *Nancy Newhall in* Paul Strand: Photographs 1915-1945, *1945*.

The world stretches wider here in New Mexico than the mind can encompass, so that to understand what it has to say the heart must be enlarged. The obvious facts of space, of distance, of brilliant sunlight, of picturesque architecture mean nothing till the walls of personality have been pushed apart. Hence to the traveler who has come to this country from a very long way off, having heard tales of spiritual wonders far more wonderful than those fabulous cities sought by Spanish conquerors, everything is a blank, nothing speaks, all the would-be voices mutter with stricken tongues. . . .

After fruitless seeking and longing to know what New Mexico is, what terrible secret of existence lurks in these starved mesas and rough-hewn canyons, in these coldly impersonal mountain ranges, one finds an answer, a voice speaking in deeply personal and convincing tones of what it has sought here, of what it has found. The material is simple and essential, those elements that the heart has to be wide indeed to hold; the medium unhackneyed and unpretentious, the result spontaneous and direct communication between man and nature and again man.

To say that this answer is found in the photographs of Paul Strand is to take for granted that man's significance lies in the depth, the intensity, the personalness, the honesty of his perceptions and actions; and the ground is prepared for at least a partial understanding of this aloof and miraculous country, as seen through one man's art. . . . *Elizabeth McCausland,* Taos, *1931.*

This search for the fundamentals that shape the character of all that rises from a land and its people reaches symphonic proportions in the New Mexico series. . . . Among the shouldering adobe forms, the buttressed apse of the Ranchos de Taos church appears again and again in magically changing lights. In the ghost towns, Aspen, St. Elmo, Red River, Strand saw the last vestiges of the frontier. *Nancy Newhall in* Paul Strand: Photographs 1915-1945, *1945.*

From New Mexico, Strand drove down to Mexico. Here it was the spirit of the people—their grace, their pride, and their enduring strength—that moved him. Returning to the "candid" theme of nearly twenty years earlier, he fitted a prism on the lens of his 5″ x 7″ Graflex (always masked to 5″ x 6¼″) and went into the streets and marketplaces of the little towns. Photographed against walls under the open sky, sometimes gently revealed, sometimes struck with vivid sunlight, these portraits attain a massive solidity and intensity that recall the work of Hill. In the dark churches, Strand found the bultos, strange images of Christ and the Virgin, which seem to symbolize, like the brief glimpses of the land and the architecture in this series, the emotional preoccupations of the people. *Nancy Newhall in* Paul Strand: Photographs 1915-1945, *1945.*

Not a great impersonal struggle is the reality of the Mexican subject matter, but the immediate urgent struggle for survival of a whole society. Behind the inscrutable faces of these men, women, and children hide centuries of labor, sorrow, and death. . . . In the photographs of bultos, the crucified Christ is the figure of every peasant broken in his daily war for bread. It is possible to look at these photographs as at still lifes executed with consummate skill, or to study them as documents of the culture which created them. But this is a static approach; the terrible stillness of their plastic organization proves that behind the surface representation seethe volcanic forces. *Elizabeth McCausland in* U.S. Camera, *1940.*

Enter the ruined hacienda: see Christ
in fifty different tortured poses,
varnished, carved to semblance of life, endowed
with breath almost; here where the camera eye
restores the initial spirit, reveals
the permanence surviving death. Ferret out
a race's history in a finger's curve,
see sun-washed walls flaking to dust,
the dust to powder won by the wind;
deep gashes, rust of rain and sun,
stones fallen, and the black deep grooves
where peons crucified conquistadors,
nailed them to walls, whips clutched
in paralyzed hands tense in agony.

See too the solitary mare
grazing in the barbed enclosure surrounding
the dead mansion of glory, and the mountains
rising beyond, and the pendant clouds
hung in the skies, identical with
horizons Coronado never conquered.
Marks of boots and fingerprint remain
on the rainless scene; nails jut from walls
long cleaned by wind and bird of flesh and bone.
See here, a continent away, the evidence
of grandeur ground to death by time and man,
and the lonely spirit, sun on the anguished eyes
of the carved Christ; and the deep patience
men of another century engraved
on these stone walls and images—lines like words
shouting: "We are enslaved!"
                    lines in prophetic
thunder: "We shall rise,
                    conquerors."

Edwin Rolfe, Prophecy in Stone (on a Photograph by Paul
Strand), *1951*.

Our Mexican pictorial movement with its plastic concepts and new realism in open rebellion against formalism took as its basis Man, the physical world in which he moves, struggles, and dies.

Paul Strand coming to Mexico in 1932 with his creative scope penetrated the terrain of moving pictures with an unquestionable documentary and technical power. Like Sergei Eisenstein, who preceded him, Strand made an outstanding contribution with his film *Redes,* a film of dynamic realism, emotional intensity, and social outlook. It is a masterpiece, a classic of the Mexican and by extension of the Latin American milieu. This is equally true of the photographs which make up his *Mexican Portfolio.*

Strand's point of view paralleled that of the pioneers of Mexican mural painting in their opposition to formalism. Both as a film maker and as a still photographer he has continued to develop his fundamentally humanist vision in later works produced in the United States and in many other parts of the world.

I wish to pay homage to the greatness of this "American-Mexican," or better, this citizen of the world, whose work has illuminated the most objective art of our time. *David Alfaro Siqueiros in the Preface,* The Mexican Portfolio, *1967.*

For nearly ten years, Strand concentrated on films. . . . It was with joy that he returned to photography. In the fall and winter of 1943-1944, he went to Vermont. Here, as in the Gaspé, in Mexico, and New Mexico, where generations of painters and photographers have found only the superficial and the picturesque, Strand reached into the essence of New England. The shuttered white church stands on patches of snow like the terrifying grip of an ideal. In the worn doorlatch, the tar-paper patch, the crazy window among rotting clapboards, appear the ancient precision and mordant decay of New England. In the glimpse of delicate woods in snow through the side of a shed, he expressed its frail and stubborn loveliness. The portrait of the old farmer, Mr. Bennett, is one of the most eloquent and poignant in photography. *Nancy Newhall in* Paul Strand: Photographs 1915-1945, *1945*.

New England has and I think will always have a special meaning for Americans. The land and its people, their cities and towns, their factories and mills, the villages surrounded by farms, the long coast and the sea whipping against it—all these are New England. But there is something more. For here in this region, in these six states of the Union, were born many of the thoughts and actions that have shaped America for more than three hundred years.

From the very start, New England was a battleground where intolerance and tolerance faced each other over religious minorities, over trials for witchcraft, over the abolitionists. The freedom of the individual to think, to believe, and to speak freely was an issue fought out here more than once. The rights of man were here affirmed in 1775 and 1860. Men gave their lives in the struggle against political tyranny, and when it took courage to speak out against human slavery in the face of obloquy and the threat of mob violence, they spoke out. The voices of Roger Williams, Ethan Allen, Samuel Adams, and James Otis; of Garrison, Wendell Phillips, and John Brown; of Thoreau, Emerson, and many others, true spokesmen of America in their time, echoed in the air of these states.

It was this concept of New England that led me to try to find in present-day New England images of nature and architecture and faces of people that were either part of or related in feeling to its great tradition. *Paul Strand in the Photographer's Foreword,* Time in New England, *1950.*

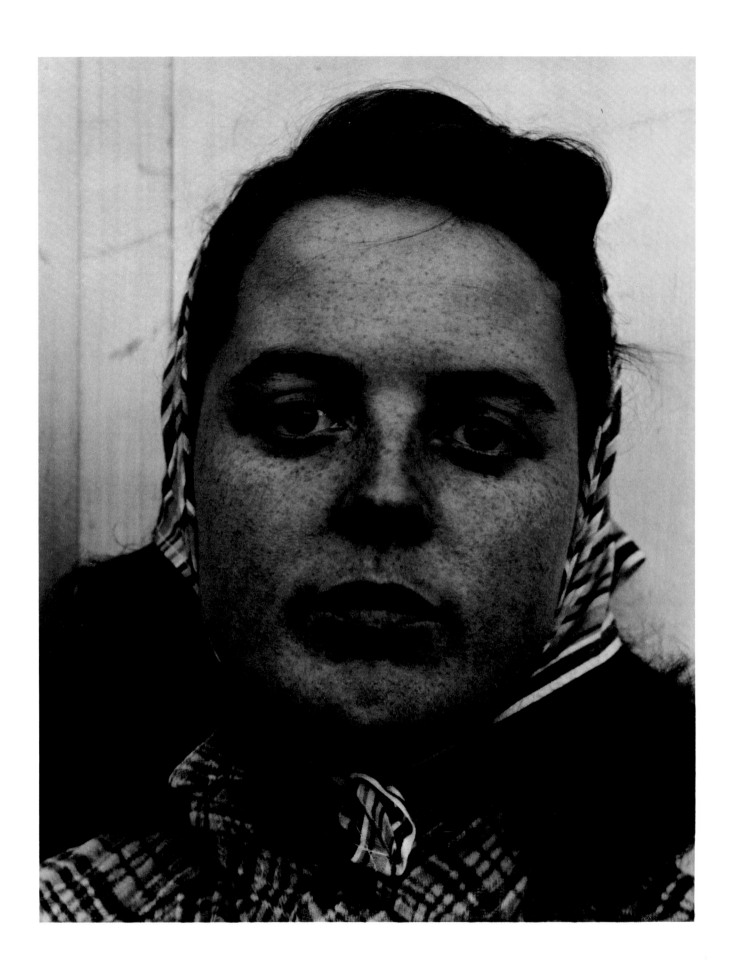

Gradually there unfolded that honest and intense vision which he defined as essential to photography. As he grew older, Paul Strand would become more prolific, because he became surer of his purpose; yet painfully and slowly he felt his way through the world of sight, measuring progress not by thousands of photographs taken, but by quintessence of experience captured in one print. This tempo is characteristic of one kind of creative temperament, which grows as slowly as a century plant to produce one prodigious flower. *Elizabeth McCausland in* U.S. Camera, *1940.*